Pathways to Artistry

A Method for Comprehensive Technical and Musical Development

Catherine Rollin

TECHNIQUE

1

The goal of the *Pathways to Artistry* series is to emphasize the importance of technique and artistry beginning at the early stages of piano study. There are two books at each level of the series—*Technique* and *Repertoire.* Students can use them as soon as they have attained basic reading skills. The *Technique* books help students develop and understand the physical skills needed to play music artistically and with technical assurance. The *Repertoire* books bridge the gap between the early levels of method books and intermediate masterwork repertoire. Written to develop specific skills, the original music that I wrote for the *Repertoire* books will foster an appreciation for the sound and styles of masterworks while incorporating the physical vocabulary attained through the *Technique* books.

Good technique and musical artistry are inseparable. Their mastery is often a lifetime quest. It is my hope that through this series students will find themselves on the pathway to that goal.

Catherine Rollin

I would like to express my heartfelt appreciation to E. L. Lancaster for his input on the Pathways to Artistry Series. He helped me organize and convey in print an approach to developing artistry that is central to my teaching.

CONTENTS

HOW TO USE THE SERIES

The *Pathways to Artistry* Series can be used:

- **As a method:** Once students have acquired basic reading skills, *Pathways to Artistry Technique Book 1* and *Repertoire Book 1* can replace the instructional method book.

- **With a method:** *Pathways to Artistry Technique Book 1* and *Repertoire Book 1* can be used in conjunction with another method to reinforce reading skills and expose students to the sounds, technique, style, form and artistic ideas in the *Pathways to Artistry* series.

If students have not used this series as part of their early training, *Technique Book 1* is recommended for transfer students at more advanced levels.

About *Pathways to Artistry* Technique Book 1

Technique Book 1 can be introduced as soon as students have acquired basic reading skills. By progressing through the book unit by unit, they develop an extensive *physical vocabulary*, and a *verbal vocabulary* to describe the physical skills. Teachers and students find it easy to communicate when they have a shared vocabulary to clearly express the desired physical approach to the piano.

This book is divided into five units and a coda.

Units 1 and 2 introduce and explain 12 basic skills for pianists. These important physical skills are codified, named and explained using a three-step process for learning to execute them.

Unit 3 introduces five-finger patterns, chords and accompaniment patterns. Understanding these patterns and being able to play them in many keys helps students gain familiarity with keyboard topography. Repetitions through written-out transpositions build physical assurance.

Units 4 and 5 include exercises that use the skills introduced in the first two units. These exercises apply the skills to the patterns and chords from Unit 3 and students transpose them to selected keys.

Coda—These reference pages summarize the basic skills, patterns and chords.

How to Use *Pathways to Artistry* Technique Book 1

Students should first develop each of the 12 basic skills introduced in Units 1 and 2 until they become part of their physical vocabulary. To fully concentrate on each new skill, hands separate practice is advised first—followed by hands together when appropriate. **Strong Fingers** (page 7) are required to maintain a good hand position as well as even tone and steady rhythm. This skill should be incorporated into all exercises.

After transposition is introduced (page 23), exercises are written beginning on C and continuing to the C an octave higher. Students should play all of the positions to build keyboard assurance and reinforce each pattern; however, teachers may assign fewer positions.

The Three R's:
Return, Review and Reinforce

The 12 basic skills presented in *Pathways to Artistry, Technique Book 1*, are used in all levels of music. Once students have gone through the entire book, they should **return** to **review** and **reinforce** skills as the need for them arises in their music.

THE PERFECT POSITION AT THE PIANO

A good pianist is a combination of musical artist and athlete. Like athletes who participate in sports and make "great plays," pianists must train and condition themselves to play greatly! The perfect position at the piano involves:

- good posture
- proper seating height
- correct distance from the keyboard
- good hand position

The following descriptions will help you develop the perfect position at the piano. Starting out with good form is crucial to developing good technic.

Posture

- Sit tall, with good support in the lower back.
- Lean slightly forward from the hip so that the weight of the torso is toward the keyboard.

Check Yourself

Are you sitting tall, with your upper torso leaning comfortably toward the keyboard?

Height

Sit at a height where:

- the shoulders are relaxed
- the forearms fall comfortably at a level with the keys
- the elbows can swing freely

Your feet should be firmly on the floor. If you cannot reach the floor with your feet, use a pedal assist or adjustable footstool. Otherwise, keep the feet crossed at the ankles so they will not dangle.

Check Yourself

Is your forearm higher or lower than the keys? If so, you are sitting either too high or too low and should adjust the height of the bench.

THE PERFECT POSITION AT THE PIANO

Distance

Sit far enough from the keyboard so that the arms have freedom.

Check Yourself

Can you stretch out your arms and touch the fallboard with the second joint of the fingers? If you cannot stretch out your arms, you are sitting too close.

Hand Position

- Stand up and allow your hands to fall freely at your side.

- In a seated position, maintain this relaxed, natural position and place one hand at a time on the keyboard.

- The thumb should lie on its side, and fingers 2, 3, 4 and 5 should fall in a natural curve. The fingers should maintain this natural curve as you play.

- Keeping the fingers in this position makes the knuckles form what looks like a bridge.

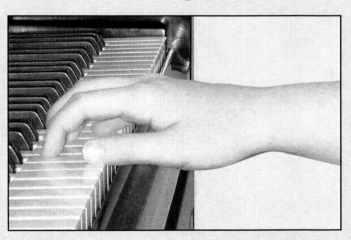

Check Yourself

Is your thumb lying on its side, without tension?
Are fingers 2, 3, 4 and 5 maintaining a natural curve?
Do the knuckles of the hand look like a bridge?

Unit One

Elastic Wrist

A flexible "elastic" wrist allows the weight from the arm to drop freely into the playing fingers, eliminating forearm tension and leading to a good tone.

Preparation before Playing

Place one hand on a tabletop or the fallboard, with fingertips near the edge. Follow the motions indicated by **bold italic** in the following three steps to feel the wrist work as a hinge. Repeat with the other hand.

Three Steps for Developing an Elastic Wrist:

A. **Lift the wrist** slightly to prepare for the drop.

B. **Drop the wrist** with the weight of the arm as the key is depressed.

C. **Lift the wrist** and arm weight out of the key as it is released.

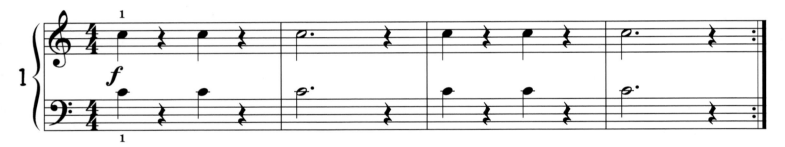

The elastic wrist is important in creating dynamics. The weight of the arm drops more for louder notes and less for softer notes. The wrist is lifted slightly higher for louder sounds.

Use the elastic wrist on every note. After each note is played, the wrist rises to prepare for the next drop.

Strong Fingers

Strong fingers make it possible to play with an even tone and a steady rhythm.

Preparation before Playing

Place the right hand on a tabletop or the fallboard, keeping the fingers curved in the natural position described on page 5. With left hand finger 2, gently exert pressure on the first segment of finger 2 of the right hand—then fingers 3, 4 and 5. To prevent the first joint from *caving in* (going concave), keep the weight of the arm focused on the playing surface of the fingertip. This focused weight creates resistance to the pressure, preventing the first joint from *caving in* or collapsing. Repeat with fingers 2, 3, 4 and 5 of the left hand, applying pressure with finger 2 of the right hand.

Three Steps for Developing Strong Fingers:

A. *Curve fingers* 2, 3, 4 and 5 to form three distinct segments divided by the joints. The fingertips should stay in contact with the keys as they are depressed with the arm weight. The thumb stays on its side.

B. *Play with the broad fingertip cushion, and with the finger a little less than a 90° angle* to the white keys. This gives the finger(s) a slightly broader playing surface than the very tip.

C. *Resist with focused weight on the first segment to prevent the fingertip joint from collapsing.* This resistance is called a "supported" first joint.

On exercises 1 and 2, use finger 2 of the hand that is not playing to put a slight amount of pressure on the finger playing the tied whole notes, checking for resistance.

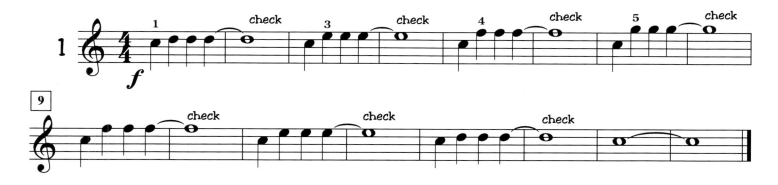

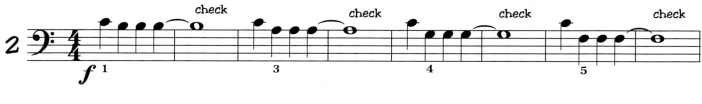

Wrist Rotation

Wrist rotation allows the weight of the arm and hand to transfer from finger to finger.

Preparation before Playing

Practice opening and closing an imaginary door handle in the air. Feel the wrist and forearm turn at the elbow hinge.

Three Steps for Developing Wrist Rotation:

A. **Lift the wrist** to prepare, then **drop the wrist** with the weight of the arm (steps 1 and 2 of the Elastic Wrist, page 6).

B. **Rotate the wrist** so the weight shifts to the next playing finger. The smaller the interval, the smaller the rotation.

C. **Lift the wrist and arm weight** out of the keys.

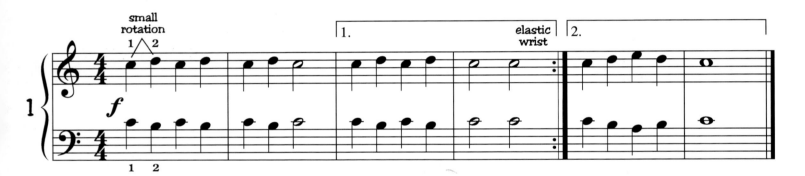

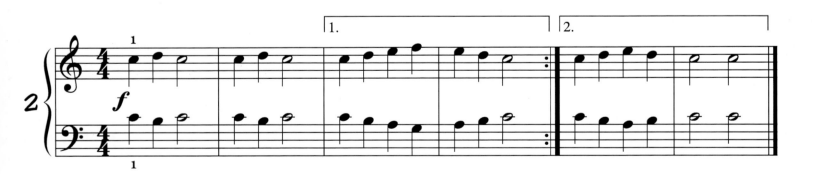

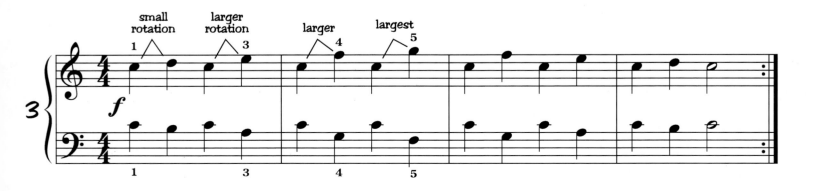

Two-Note Slurs

Two-note slurs should produce a distinctive and expressive sound. The characteristic sound is a heavier first note and lighter second note. These *distinctive sounding* two-note slurs occur between notes of equal value or a longer-shorter note pair.

Three Steps to Developing Two-Note Slurs:

A. **Lift the wrist** to prepare, as in the Elastic Wrist, page 6.

B. **Drop the weight of the arm** on the first note of the slur.

C. **Lift the wrist and arm out** on the second note of the slur.

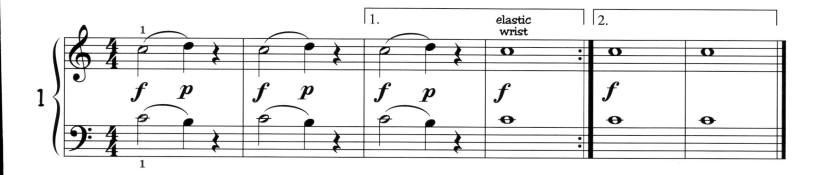

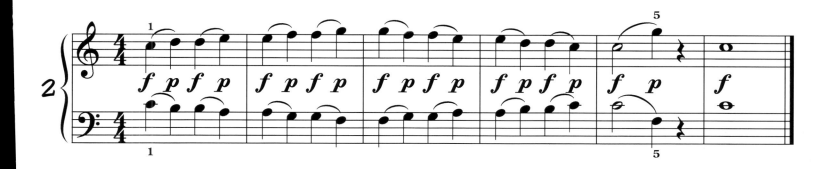

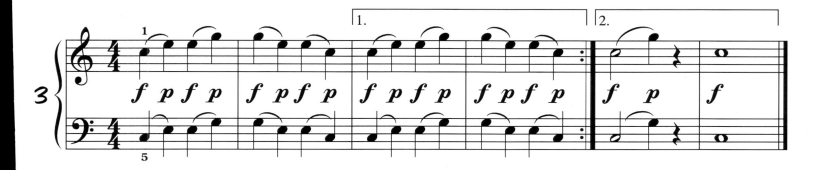

Two-note slurs do not usually have dynamics written under both notes. The heavy-light (loud-soft) concept is implied.

Balanced Torso and Forearm

A balanced torso and forearm stays in line with the hand and fingers to help create an even sound and prevent tension in the arms and upper body.

Preparation at the Piano before Playing:

Applying the three steps to developing a balanced torso and forearm (see below), place the right hand on the white keys in the center of the keyboard. Slide the whole hand up the keys to the top of the keyboard and then back down to the center. Then slide the left hand from the center to the bottom of the keyboard. Repeat with both hands sliding together to the top and bottom of the keyboard.

Three Steps for Developing a Balanced Torso and Forearm:

A. ***Align the torso and forearm to keep the weight of the arm balanced or centered over the playing fingers.*** When playing keys in front of the body, the forearm creates a straight line that is slightly diagonal to the keyboard so that the elbow does not hug the body and the weight of the forearm drops freely into the playing fingers. When playing high keys in the right hand or low keys in the left hand, the forearm forms approximately a right angle to the keyboard, allowing the weight of the arm to be centered over the playing fingers.

B. ***Lean from side to side,*** keeping the posterior in one place as you shift the weight of the torso.

C. ***Follow the playing fingers and hand with the torso and forearm.***

Use an elastic wrist and strong fingers as you play.

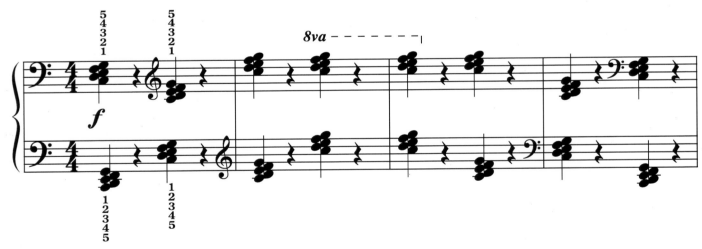

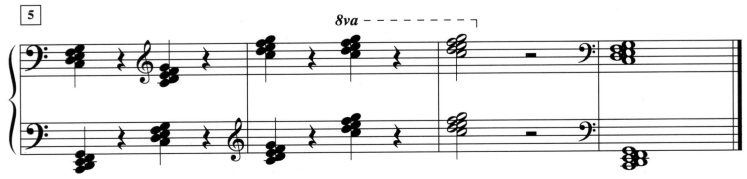

Finger Independence

Finger independence is the skill of doing one thing with one finger and something else with a different finger of the same hand at the same time.

Three Steps for Developing Finger Independence:

A. ***Practice hands separately*** first.

B. ***Practice hands together slowly.***

C. ***Be patient!*** Developing the brain connections for finger independence takes time.

On numbers 1 and 2, use wrist rotation to shift the weight of the hand to the playing finger.

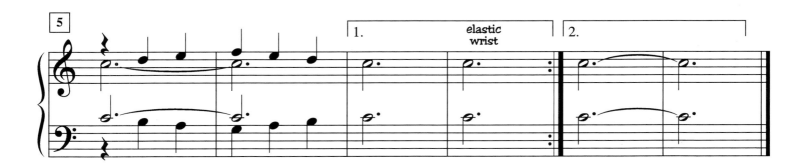

Unit Two

Slurs

Slurs combine individual notes into larger musical ideas to give the music cohesion, expressiveness and beauty. Slurs also mean *play legato.*

Three Steps for Developing Slurs:

A. **Lift the wrist** to prepare, then **drop the wrist** with the weight of the arm (steps 1 and 2 of the Elastic Wrist, page 6).

B. **Transfer the weight of the arm to the playing fingers** with a smooth (legato), subtle motion of the wrist.

C. On the last note of the slur, **lift the wrist and arm weight out.**

Follow the direction of the pitches. The wrist shifts the weight of the hand to the right for notes that are moving higher, and to the left for notes that are moving lower.

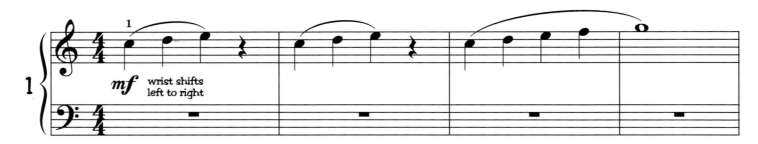

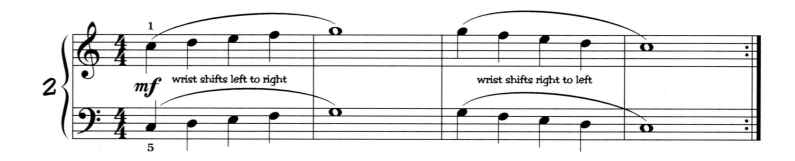

Forearm Staccato

The forearm staccato produces a lively, resonant sound.

Preparation before Playing

On a tabletop or the fallboard, practice bouncing an imaginary ball, with bounces both big and small.
Think of the forearm and hand as a unit. Do not bend at the wrist hinge.

Three Steps for Developing Forearm Staccato:

    A. ***Lift the hand*** slightly off the keys.

    B. ***Drop the weight of the hand*** into the playing finger(s). Keep the arm in motion without bending the wrist.

    C. ***Bounce out of the keys*** after they have been depressed to avoid a dull, lifeless sound.

In these exercises, bounce close to the keys for the ***p*** dynamic and *slightly* higher for the ***f*** dynamic.

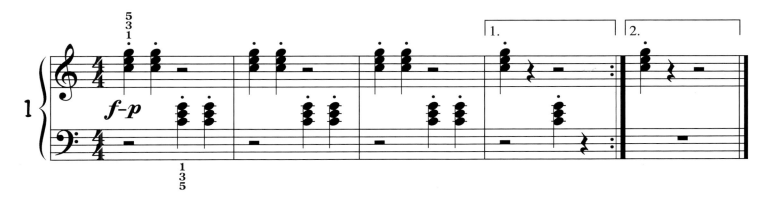

Push-Off Staccato

Push-off staccatos are used for a short, snappy sound. They are helpful for accents or sforzandos that are played staccato.

Three Steps for Developing Push-Off Staccato:

A. **Lift the wrist** slightly, to prepare for the drop.

B. **Drop the weight** of the arm into the playing fingers.

C. **Lift the wrist** with a fast motion, resulting in a fast rebound of the key(s) and a push-off effect on the playing finger(s). On accented notes, the wrist will lift even faster with a more sudden motion.

Use push-off staccato for all chords in exercises 1 and 2. The wrist will lift faster for the accents and sforzandos.

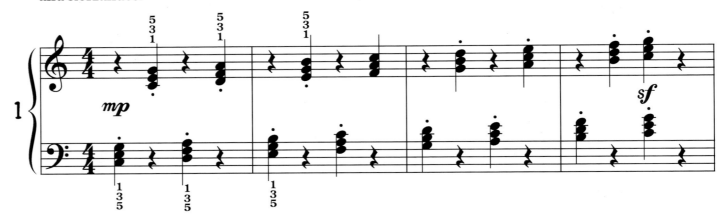

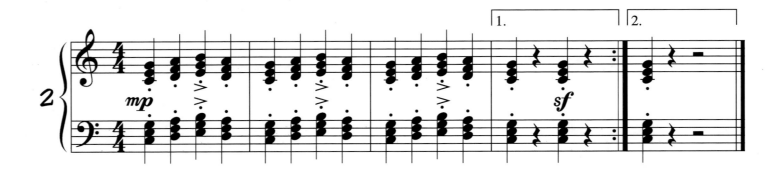

Push-Off Staccato at the End of Slurs

In exercises 1 and 2, the "push-off" note is part of a two-note slur, so it will be softer than the first note of the slur.

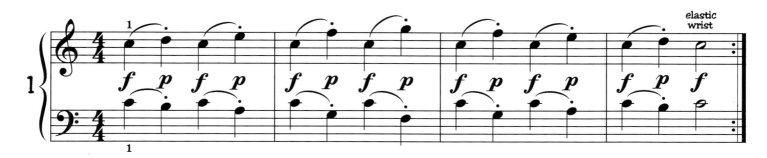

In exercises 3 and 4, the "push-off" note falls on the strong beat of the measure, so it will be louder than the first note of the slur.

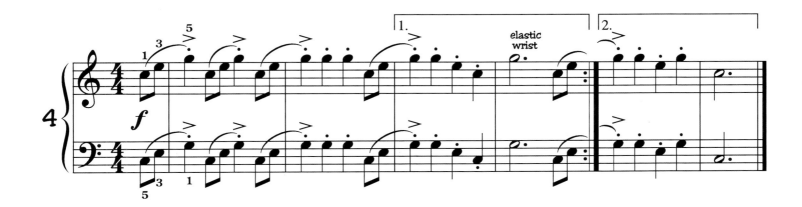

Rolling Wrist

The Rolling Wrist creates an ongoing sound in repeated circular patterns of at least three notes. As used here, it applies to patterns where the right hand moves in a counterclockwise motion and the left hand moves in a clockwise motion.

Preparation before Playing

On a tabletop or the fallboard, place the weight of the arm on the fingertip of the third finger. Using the fingertip as the axis of your circle, rotate the finger, hand, wrist and arm as one unit. Practice hands separately, with the right hand rotating counterclockwise and the left hand rotating clockwise. Repeat, using fingers 2, 4 and 5 of each hand.

Three Steps for Developing the Rolling Wrist:

A. **Lift the wrist to prepare,** then **drop the wrist** with the weight of the arm (steps 1 and 2 of the Elastic Wrist, page 6).

B. **Lift the wrist** to start the circle. The wrist moves up slightly to the right for the right hand, and up slightly to the left for the left hand.

C. **Keep the wrist in motion (rolling)** and play the subsequent notes of the pattern as the circle rounds the top. Continue the circles (rolling motion) so the sound will flow as the pattern repeats.

Arm-to-Arm Independence

Arm-to-Arm Independence is the skill of doing one motion with one arm and a different motion with the other arm at the same time.

Preparation before Playing

On a tabletop or the fallboard, practice the different motions of the following exercises, hands separately and then hands together.

Three Steps for Developing Arm-to-Arm Independence:

A. ***Practice hands separately*** at first.

B. ***Practice hands together slowly.***

C. ***Be patient!*** Developing the brain connections for arm-to-arm independence takes time.

Damper Pedal Technique*

Most pianos have three pedals. The damper pedal is the most commonly used pedal. The damper pedal raises the dampers, allowing the strings to vibrate. When the damper pedal is pressed, the whole piano resonates.

Three Steps for Developing Beginning Damper Pedal Technic:

A. **Place the ball of your right foot on the damper (right) pedal.** Keep the heel firmly on the floor.

B. **Depress the pedal** and pretend that you have "Crazy Glue" on your foot. Your foot and the pedal go up and down as one unit.

C. **Release the pedal** and see how far up it needs to go to stop the strings from vibrating. Try not to release the pedal all the way, to avoid a clunking sound.

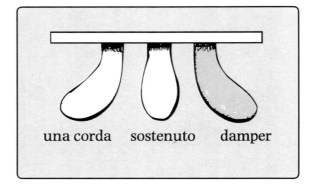

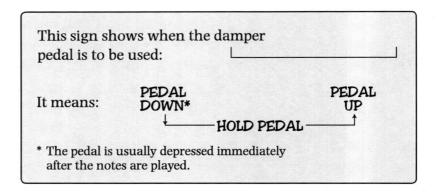

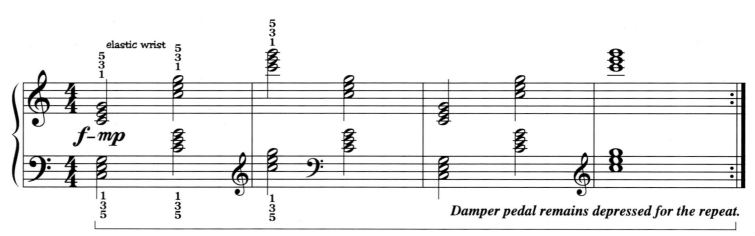

Damper pedal remains depressed for the repeat.

A fun way to learn about the grand piano's "echo chamber:"

1. Press the pedal and listen for the sound of the dampers coming off the strings.

2. Lift the pedal up to let the dampers go back down. Repeat steps 1 and 2.

3. Sing or shout above the soundboard when you hear the dampers go up on step 1. Do you hear the echo of your own voice created by the vibrating soundboard?

* "Overlapping pedal" will be introduced in *Pathways to Artistry, Technique Book 2.*

Patterns and Chords

Major Five-Finger Patterns

The major five-finger pattern is a natural and comfortable position
for playing with "the perfect hand position."

The major five-finger pattern consists of: whole step, whole step, half step, whole step.

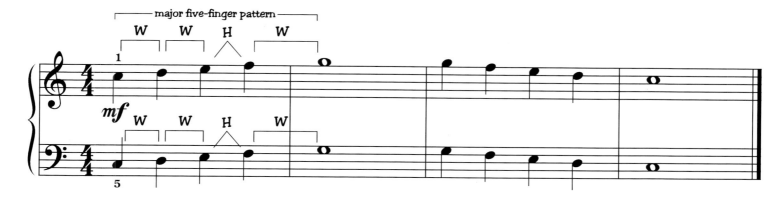

Major Triads

The major triad consists of notes 1, 3 and 5 of the major five-finger pattern.

Broken Major Triads

Notes 1, 3 and 5 of the major five-finger pattern, played separately, outline a broken major triad.

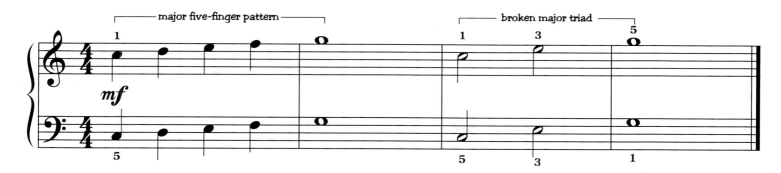

Blocked Major Triads

Notes 1, 3 and 5 of the major five-finger pattern, played together, form a blocked major triad.

Minor Five-Finger Patterns

The minor five-finger pattern lowers note 3 of the major five-finger pattern a half step.
This creates a pattern consisting of: whole step, half step, whole step, whole step.

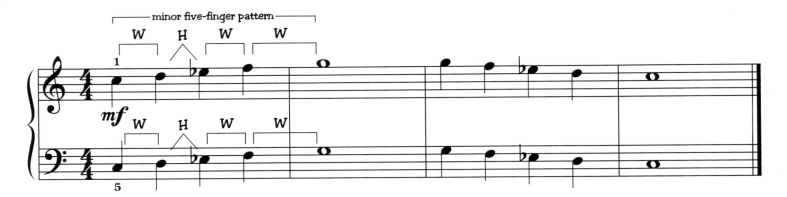

Minor Triads

The minor triad consists of notes 1, 3 and 5 of the minor five-finger pattern.

Broken Minor Triads

Notes 1, 3 and 5 of the minor five-finger pattern, played separately, outline a broken minor triad.

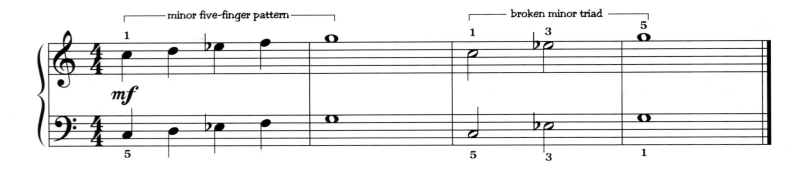

Blocked Minor Triads

Notes 1, 3 and 5 of the minor five-finger pattern, played together, form a blocked minor triad.

I and V⁷ Chords

The I Chord

The I chord is formed using notes 1, 3 and 5 of the scale.

Key of C Major

The V⁷ Chord

The **V⁷** chord is built on note 5 of the scale, using the intervals of a 3rd, 5th and 7th above it.

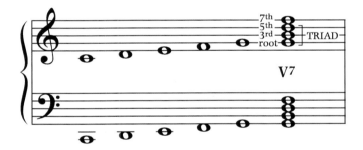

The V⁷ Chord in a Different Position

The **V⁷** chord often appears in a different position (inversion), making it possible to move smoothly to the I chord. The 5th is often omitted.

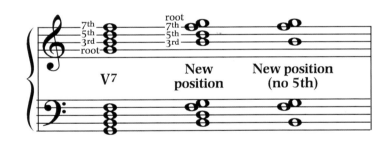

Play these **I** and **V⁷** chords.

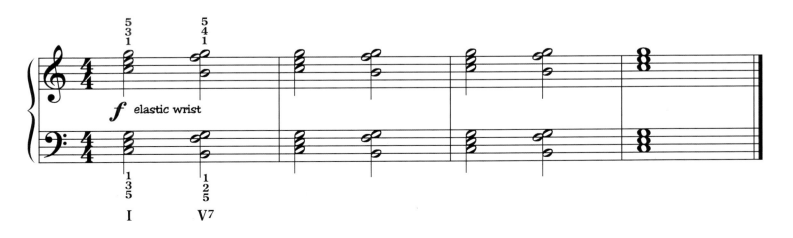

Accompaniment Patterns

In piano music, one hand often plays the melody and the other plays an accompaniment. These accompaniments are based on chords that go with the melodies. The chords are often broken in various patterns.

Two Common Accompanying Patterns

Broken Chords Using the Rolling Wrist

Keep the wrist in motion as you play.

Alberti Bass Using Wrist Rotation

One of the most common forms of broken chords is the *Alberti bass* (named for composer Domenico Alberti). This pattern uses wrist rotation and moves between the bottom, top, middle and top notes of the chord. Shift the weight of the hand to each note as you play.

The major and minor five-finger patterns and their transpositions beginning on white keys have been written on pages 23–27 as models. Starting on page 28, students transpose these patterns on their own.

These patterns are on pages 23–27.

Major Five-Finger Patterns and I–V7–I Chords Beginning on White Keys

> **Transposition**
>
> Playing a pattern at another pitch level is called *transposition*. Major and minor five-finger patterns can be played starting on different pitches, following the same patterns of half and whole steps.

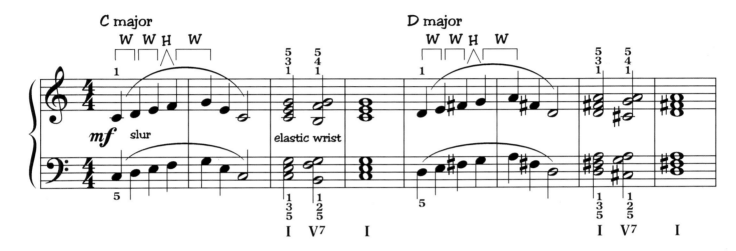

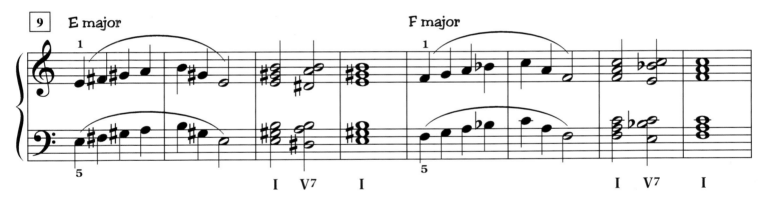

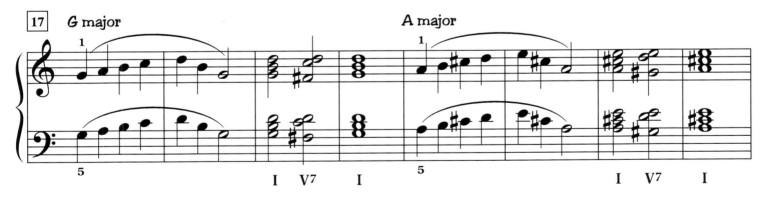

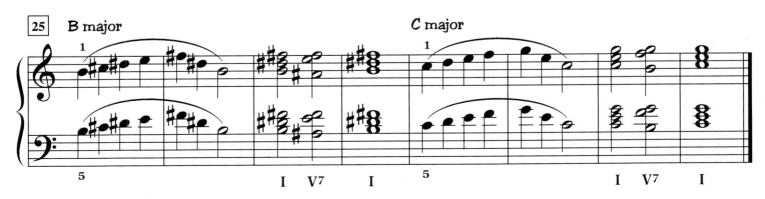

Major and Minor Five-Finger Patterns
Beginning on White Keys

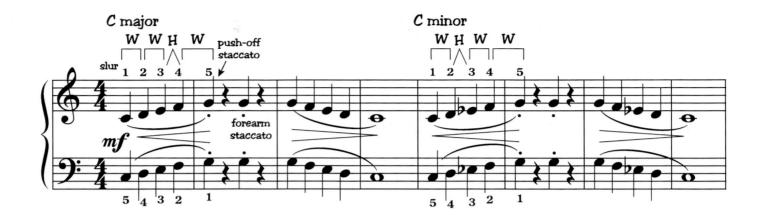

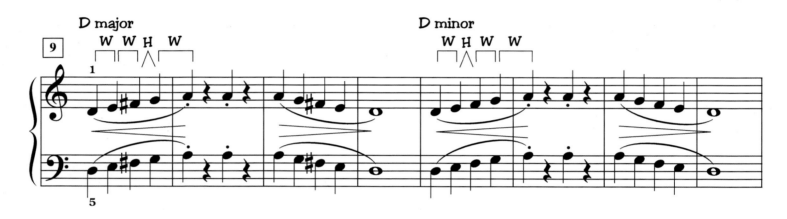

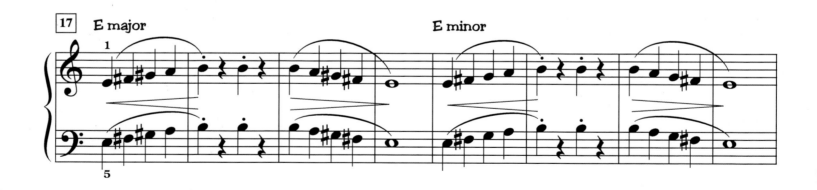

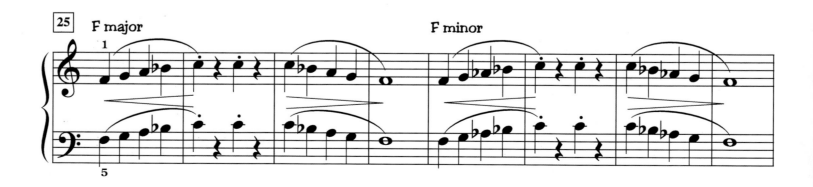

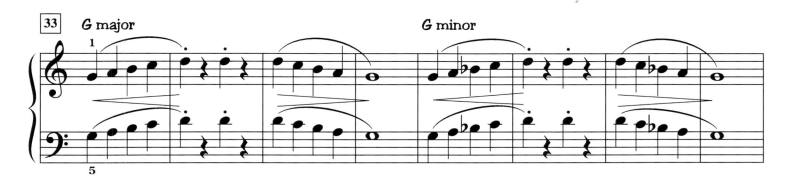

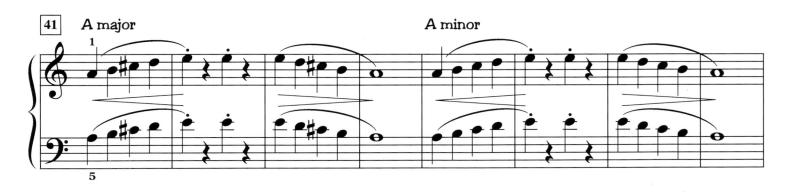

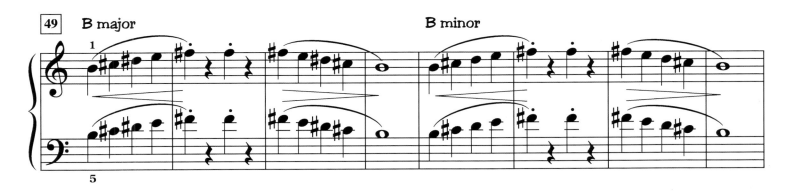

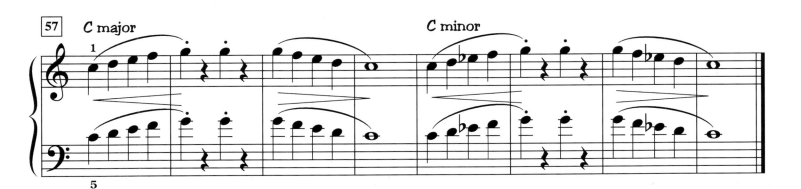

Unit Four

1. Using the Elastic Wrist

> **Remember:**
> A. *Lift the wrist* to prepare.
> B. *Drop the wrist* with the weight of the arm.
> C. *Lift the wrist* and arm weight out.

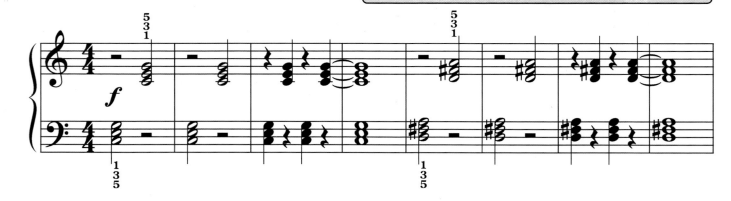

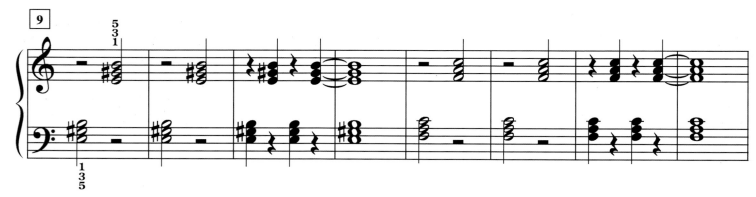

Optional: Play this page using minor triads.

2. Using Strong Fingers

> **Remember:**
> A. *Curve the fingers.*
> B. *Play with the broad fingertip cushion and with a little less than a 90° angle.*
> C. *Resist!*

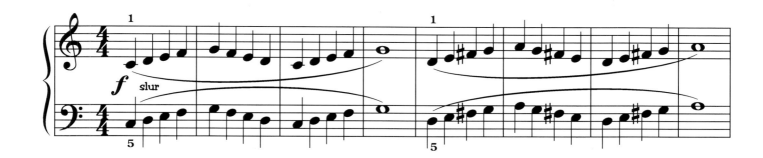

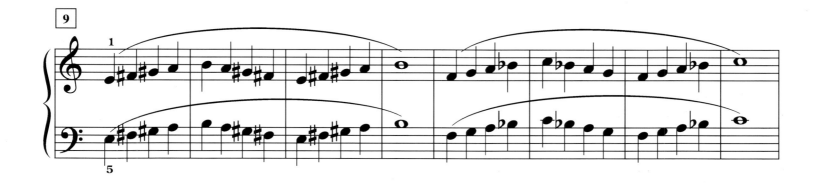

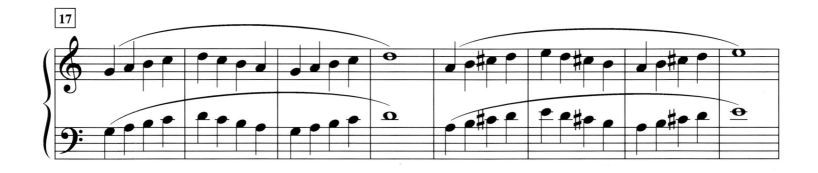

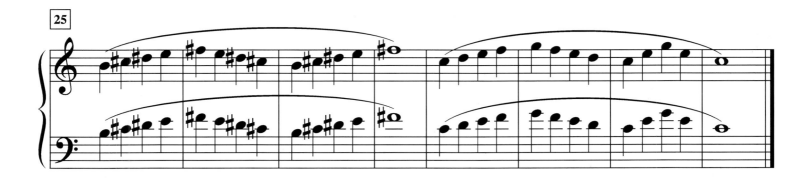

Optional: Play this page using minor five-finger patterns.

3. Using Wrist Rotation

Remember:

A. *Lift the wrist* to prepare, then *drop the wrist* with the weight of the arm.

B. *Rotate the wrist*.

C. *Lift the wrist and arm weight out*.

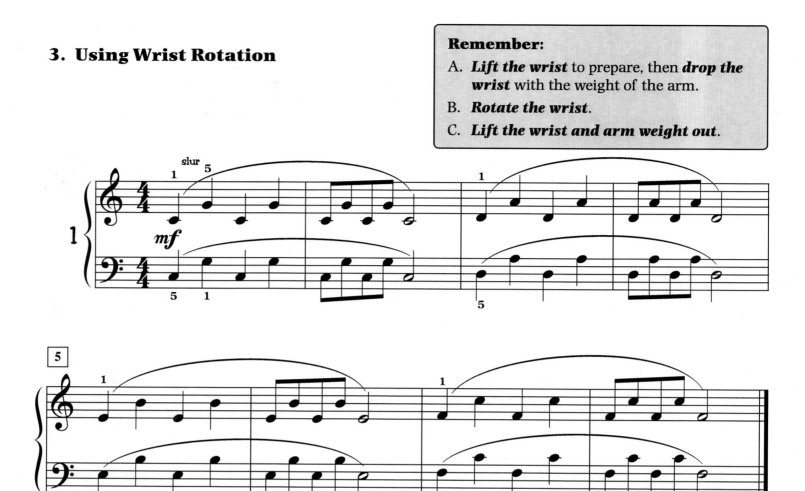

Continue with G, A, B and C major patterns.

Continue with G, A, B and C major patterns.

Optional: Play No. 2 using minor five-finger patterns.

Continue with E, F, G, A, B and C major patterns.

Optional: Play No. 3 using minor five-finger patterns.

Continue with E, F, G, A, B and C major/minor patterns.

4. Using Two-Note Slurs

> **Remember:**
> A. *Lift the wrist* to prepare.
> B. *Drop the wrist* with the weight of the arm.
> C. *Lift the wrist and arm weight out*.

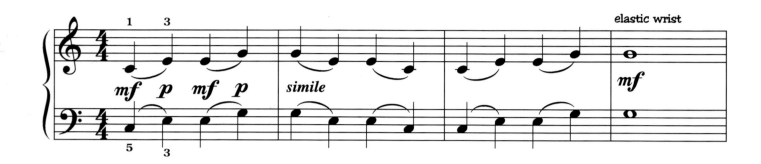

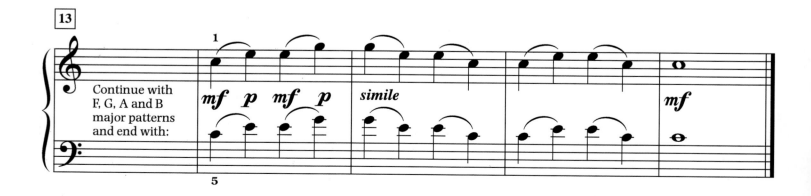

Optional: Play using minor five-finger patterns.

5. Using Balanced Torso and Forearm

> **Remember:**
> A. *Align*.
> B. *Lean*.
> C. *Follow*.

Continue with G, A, B and C major triads.

Optional: Play using minor triads.

6. Using Finger Independence

> **Remember:**
> A. *Hands separately.*
> B. *Hands together slowly.*
> C. *Be patient!*

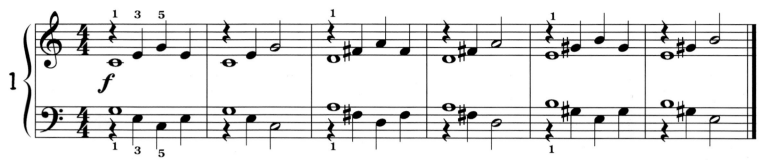

Continue with F, G, A, B and C major patterns.

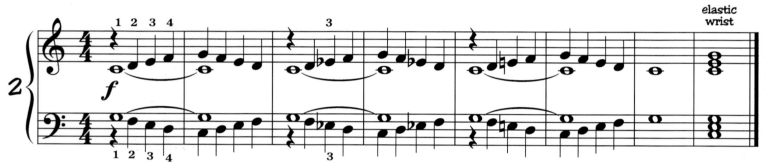

Continue with D, E, F, G, A, B and C major/minor patterns.

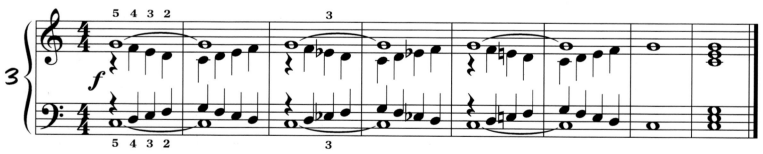

Continue with D, E, F, G, A, B and C major/minor patterns.

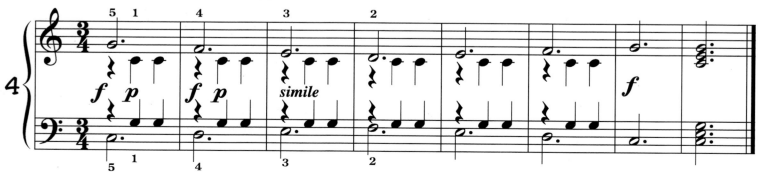

Continue with D, E, F, G, A, B and C major patterns.

Using Basic Technical Skills 7–12

Unit Five

7. Using Slurs

> **Remember:**
> A. *Lift the wrist* to prepare, then *drop the wrist* with the weight of the arm.
> B. *Transfer the weight* from finger to finger.
> C. *Lift the wrist* and arm weight out.

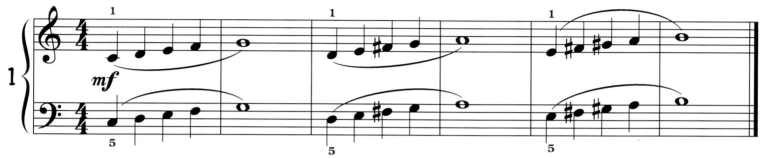

Continue with F, G, A, B and C major patterns.

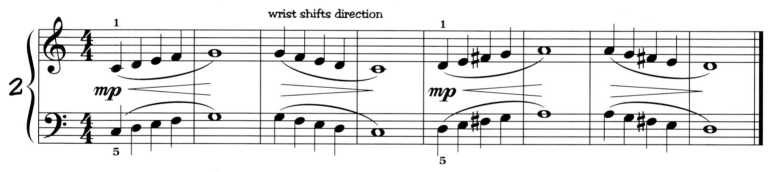

Continue with E, F, G, A, B and C major patterns.

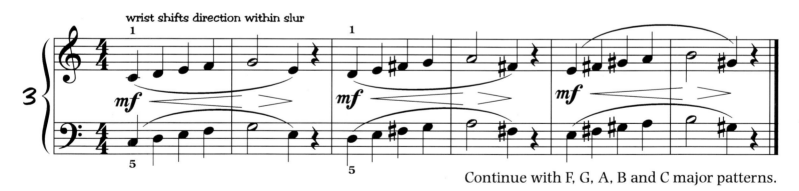

Continue with F, G, A, B and C major patterns.

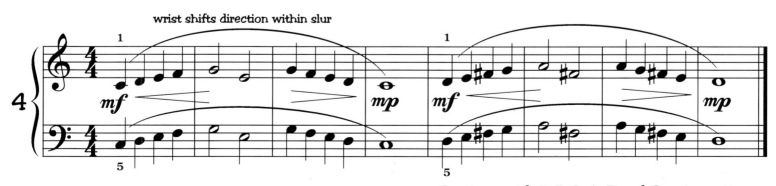

Continue with E, F, G, A, B and C major patterns.

Optional: Play this page using minor five-finger patterns.

8. Using Forearm Staccato

Remember:

A. **Lift the hand** slightly off the keys.

B. **Drop weight** with the hand and forearm as one unit, keeping the arm in motion.

C. **Bounce** out.

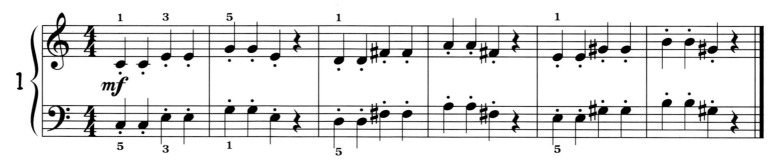

Continue with F, G, A, B and C major patterns.

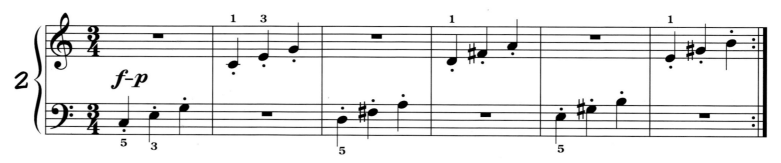

Continue with F, G, A, B and C major patterns.

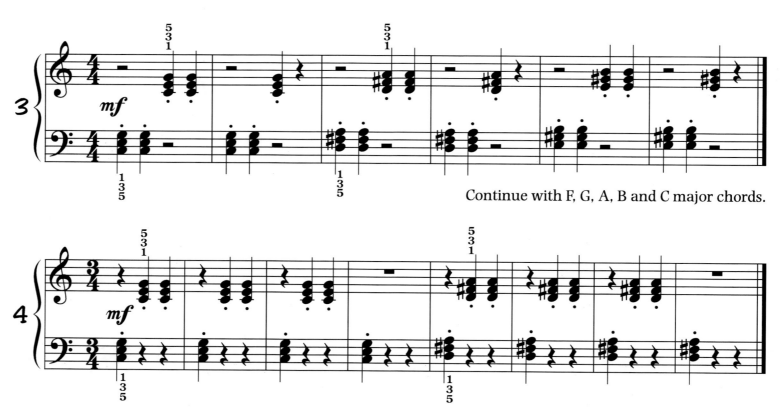

Continue with F, G, A, B and C major chords.

Continue with E, F, G, A, B and C major chords.

Optional: Play this page using minor five-finger patterns and chords.

9. Using Push-Off Staccato

Continue all exercises with F, G, A, B and C major chords and patterns.

> **Remember:**
> A. ***Lift the wrist*** to prepare.
> B. ***Drop the weight*** of the arm into the playing fingers.
> C. ***Lift the wrist*** with a fast motion.

Optional: Play this page using minor five-finger chords and patterns.

10. Using the Rolling Wrist

Continue both exercises with G, A, B and C major patterns.

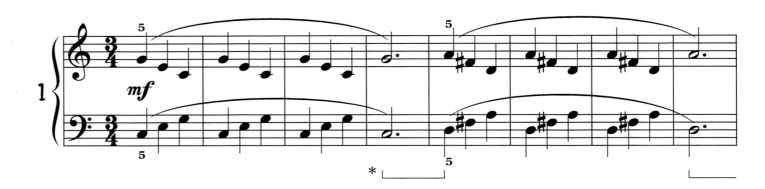

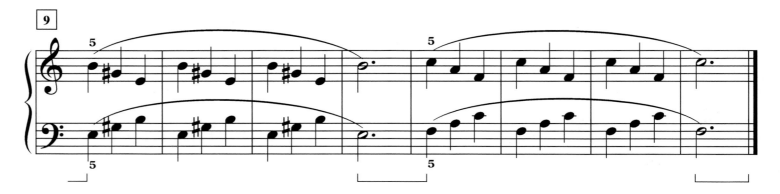

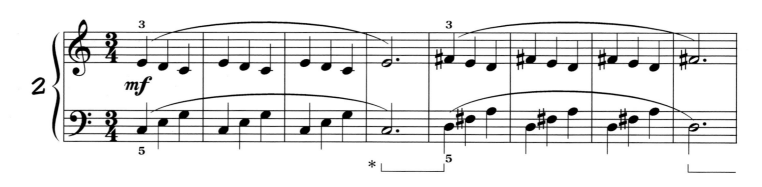

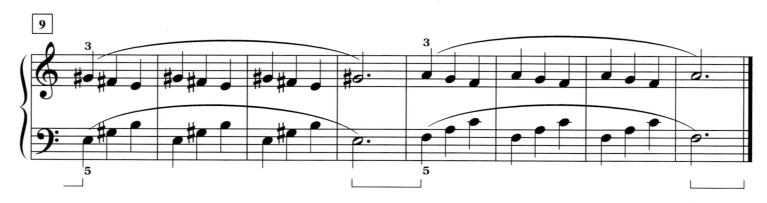

*Pedal is optional—if used, release at the beginning of each new pattern.

11. Using Arm-to-Arm Independence

> **Remember:**
> A. *Hands separately.*
> B. *Hands together slowly.*
> C. *Be patient!*

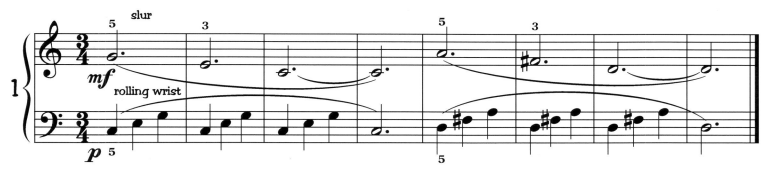

Continue with E, F, G, A, B and C major patterns.

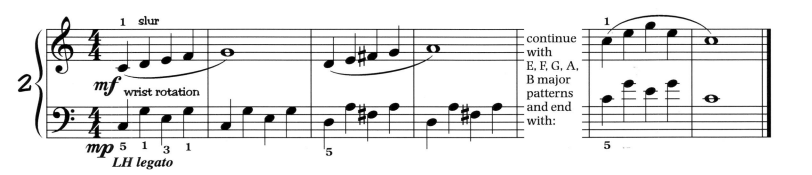

continue with E, F, G, A, B major patterns and end with:

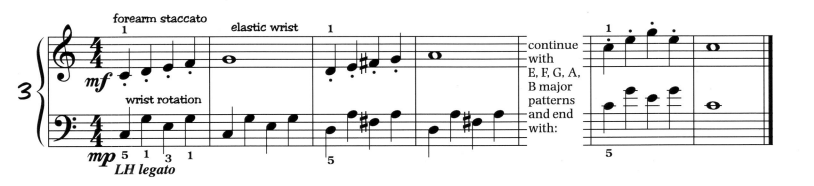

continue with E, F, G, A, B major patterns and end with:

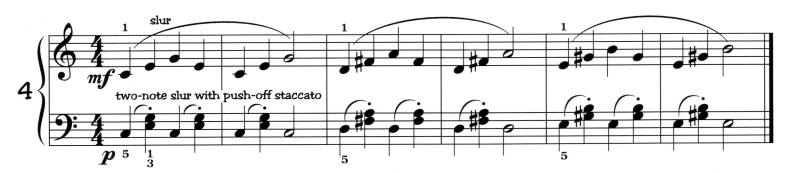

Continue with F, G, A, B and C major patterns.

12. Using the Damper Pedal

Play both exercises with other

dynamics: *p*, *mp*, *mf*, *ff*.

Continue with G, A, B and C major chords.

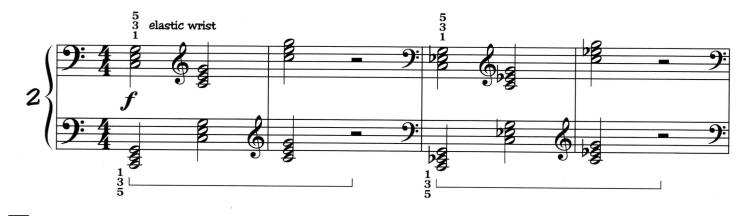

Continue with E, F, G, A, B and C major and minor chords.

Technical Index—The 12 Basic Technical Skills   Coda

1. **Elastic Wrist** (page 6)
   A. *Lift the wrist* to prepare.
   B. *Drop the wrist* with the weight of the arm.
   C. *Lift the wrist* and arm weight out.

2. **Strong Fingers** (page 7)
   A. *Curve the fingers*.
   B. *Play with the broad fingertip cushion, and with a little less than a 90° angle*.
   C. *Resist!*

3. **Wrist Rotation** (page 8)
   A. *Lift the wrist* to prepare, then *drop the wrist* with the weight of the arm.
   B. *Rotate the wrist*.
   C. *Lift the wrist* and arm weight out.

4. **Two-Note Slurs** (page 9)
   A. *Lift the wrist* to prepare.
   B. *Drop the wrist* with the weight of the arm.
   C. *Lift the wrist and arm weight out.*

5. **Balancing Torso and Forearm** (page 10)
   A. *Align.*
   B. *Lean.*
   C. *Follow.*

6. **Finger Independence** (page 11)
   A. *Hands separately.*
   B. *Hands together slowly.*
   C. *Be patient!*

7. **Slurs** (page 12)
   A. *Lift the wrist* to prepare, then *drop the wrist* with the weight of the arm.
   B. *Transfer the weight* from finger to finger.
   C. *Lift the wrist* and arm weight out.

8. **Forearm Staccato** (page 13)
   A. *Lift the hand* slightly off the keys.
   B. *Drop weight* with the hand and forearm as one unit, keeping the arm in motion.
   C. *Bounce* out.

9. **Push-Off Staccato** (page 14)
   A. *Lift the wrist* to prepare.
   B. *Drop the weight* of the arm into the playing fingers.
   C. *Lift the wrist* with a fast motion.

10. **Rolling Wrist** (page 16)
    A. *Lift the wrist* to prepare, then *drop the wrist* with the weight of the arm.
    B. *Lift the wrist* to start the circle.
    C. *Keep the wrist in motion (rolling).*

11. **Arm-to-Arm Independence** (page 17)
    A. *Hands separately.*
    B. *Hands together slowly.*
    C. *Be patient!*

12. **Damper Pedal Technique** (page 18)
    A. *Place* the ball of the foot on the damper pedal, heel firmly on the floor.
    B. *Depress* the foot and pedal as one unit.
    C. *Release* the pedal.

Patterns and Chords

Patterns

Major Five-Finger Pattern

Whole step, whole step, half step, whole step

Minor Five-Finger Pattern

Whole step, half step, whole step, whole step

Chords

Major Triad

Notes 1, 3 and 5 of the major five-finger pattern.

Minor Triad

Notes 1, 3 and 5 of the minor five-finger pattern.

I Chord

Notes 1, 3 and 5 of the scale.

V7 Chord

A chord built on the fifth note of the scale, using the intervals of a 3rd, 5th and 7th above it. It is often inverted and simplified to a three-note chord.

Accompaniment Patterns

Broken Chords using Rolling Wrist

An accompaniment pattern with a circular motion.

Alberti Bass

An accompaniment pattern that uses wrist rotation between the bottom, top, middle and top notes of the chord.